W9-DEE-625

A Note to Parents

DK READERS is a compelling program for beginning readers, designed in conjunction with leading literacy experts, including Dr. Linda Gambrell, Distinguished Professor of Education at Clemson University. Dr. Gambrell has served as President of the National Reading Conference, the College Reading Association, and the International Reading Association.

Beautiful illustrations and superb full-color photographs combine with engaging, easy-to-read stories to offer a fresh approach to each subject in the series. Each DK READER is guaranteed to capture a child's interest while developing his or her reading skills, general knowledge, and love of reading.

The five levels of DK READERS are aimed at different reading abilities, enabling you to choose the books that are exactly right for your child:

Pre-level 1: Learning to read
Level 1: Beginning to read
Level 2: Beginning to read alone
Level 3: Reading alone
Level 4: Proficient readers

The "normal" age at which a child begins to read can be anywhere from three to eight years old. Adult participation through the lower levels is very helpful for providing encouragement, discussing storylines, and sounding out unfamiliar words.

No matter which level you select, you can be sure that you are helping your child learn to read, then read to learn!

LONDON, NEW YORK, MUNICH,
MELBOURNE, and DELHI

Series Editor Penny Smith
Art Editor Leah Germann
U.S. Editors Elizabeth Hester, John Searcy
DTP Designer Almudena Díaz
Production Angela Graef
Picture Research Myriam Megharbi
Dinosaur Consultant Dougal Dixon

Reading Consultant
Linda Gambrell, Ph.D.

First American Edition, 2006
This edition, 2012
12 13 14 15 16 10 9 8 7 6 5 4 3 2 1
Published in the United States by DK Publishing, Inc.
375 Hudson Street, New York, New York 10014

DK books are available at special discounts for bulk purchases for sale
promotions, premiums, fundraising, or educational use. For details, contact:
DK Publishing Special Markets
375 Hudson Street, New York, NY 10014
SpecialSales@dk.com

A catalog record for this book is available
from the Library of Congress

ISBN: 978-0-7566-9293-3 (pb)
ISBN: 978-0-7566-9292-6 (plc)

Color reproduction by Colourscan, Singapore
Printed and bound in China by L Rex Printing Co., Ltd.

The publisher would like to thank the following for their kind permission
to reproduce their photographs:
a=above; c=center; b=below; l=left; r=right; t=top; b/g=background

Alamy Images: Robert Harding Picture Library Ltd 20-21 b/g, 31cr b/g. **Corbis:**
Matt Brown 26-27 b/g; Larry Lee Photography 18-19 b/g, 30cl b/g; W. Wayne
Lockwood, MD 4-5c b/g, 8-9 b/g; Charles Mauzy 5tcl b/g, 24-25 b/g; Craig
Tuttle 4br b/g, 14-15 b/g, 16-17 b/g, 28-29 b/g, 31bcl b/g; Jim Zuckerman 6-7,
30cb b/g. **DK Images:** Jon Hughes 4-5c, 8-9. **Getty Images:** J.P. Nacivet 22-23
b/g, 31tr b/g; James Randklev 4c b/g, 10-11 b/g.

All other images © Dorling Kindersley
For more information see: www.dkimages.com

Discover more at
www.dk.com

READERS

LEARNING
TO READ
pre-level
1

Meet the Dinosaurs

DK Publishing

Watch out!
Here come
the dinosaurs.

4

Here is the scary Tyrannosaurus [tie-RAN-uh-SORE-us]. It has sharp teeth.

Tyrannosaurus

teeth

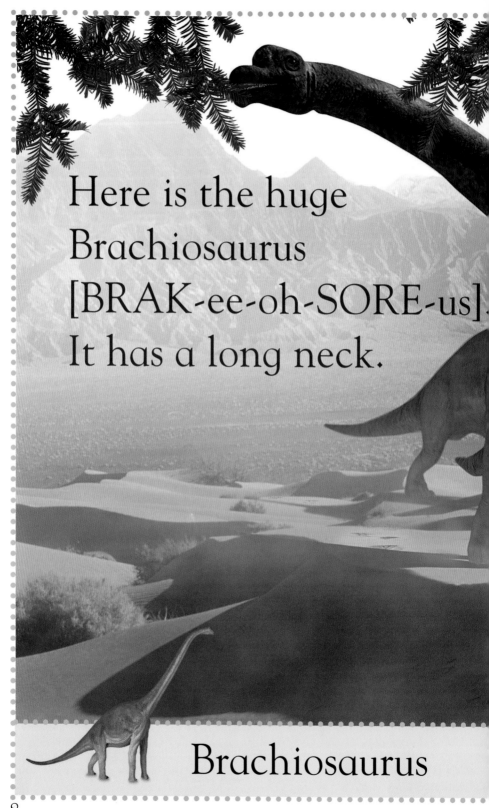

Here is the huge
Brachiosaurus
[BRAK-ee-oh-SORE-us].
It has a long neck.

Brachiosaurus

neck

Here is the tough
Triceratops
[try-SAIR-uh-tops].
It has three horns.

Triceratops

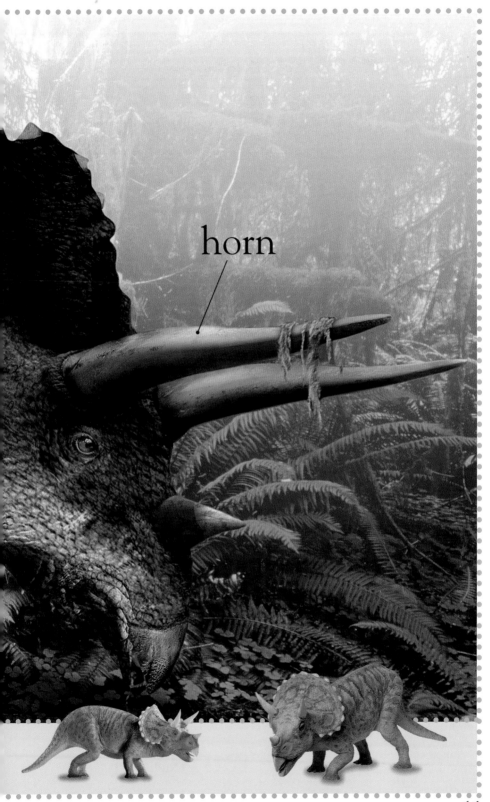

horn

Here is the fierce
Velociraptor
[vuh-LOSS-uh-rap-ter].
It has sharp claws.

Velociraptor

claw

crest

Corythosaurus

Here is the noisy
Corythosaurus
[ko-RITH-oh-SORE-us].
It has a bright crest.

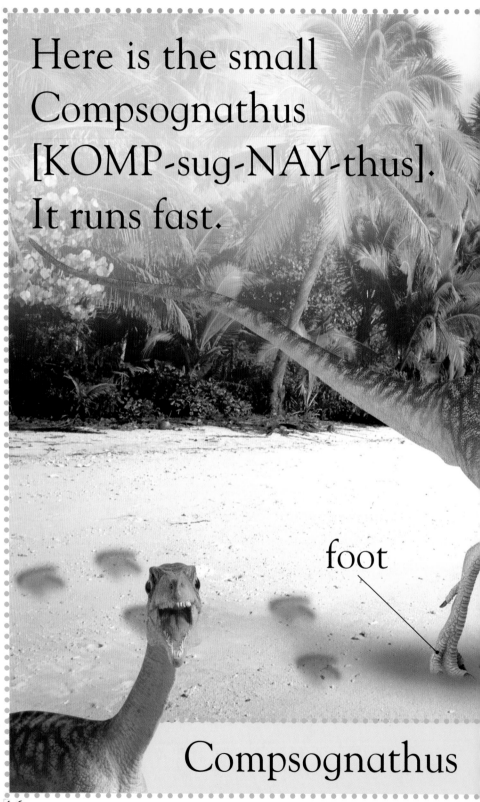

Here is the small Compsognathus [KOMP-sug-NAY-thus]. It runs fast.

foot

Compsognathus

16

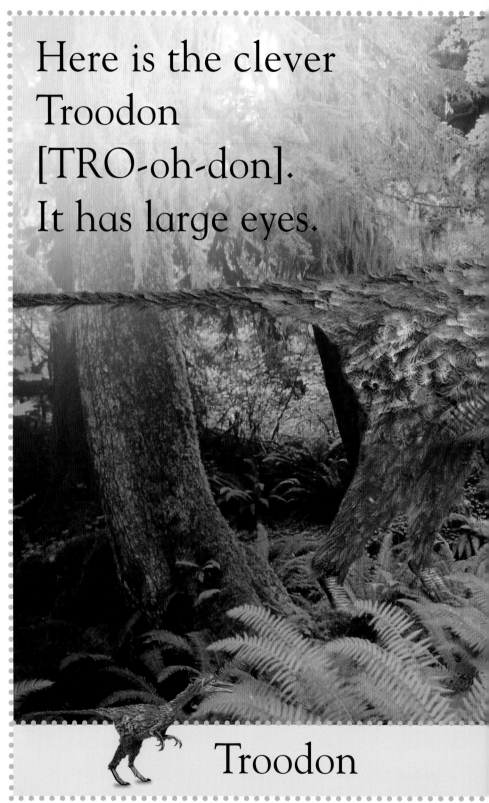

Here is the clever
Troodon
[TRO-oh-don].
It has large eyes.

Troodon

eye

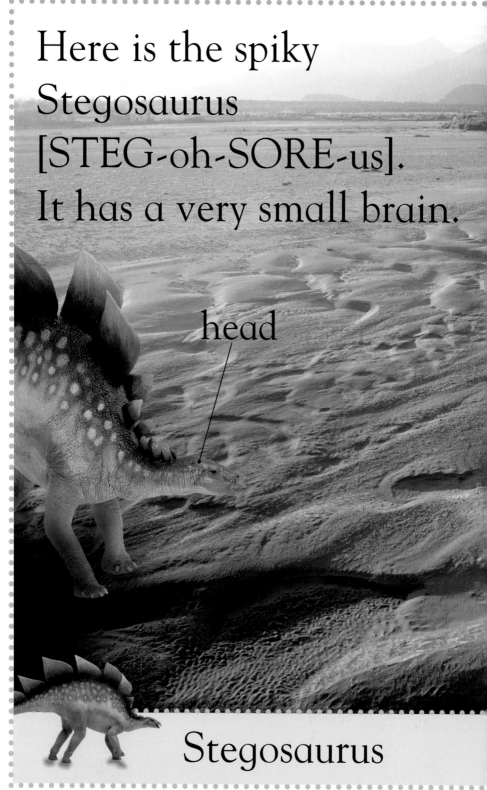

Here is the spiky
Stegosaurus
[STEG-oh-SORE-us].
It has a very small brain.

head

Stegosaurus

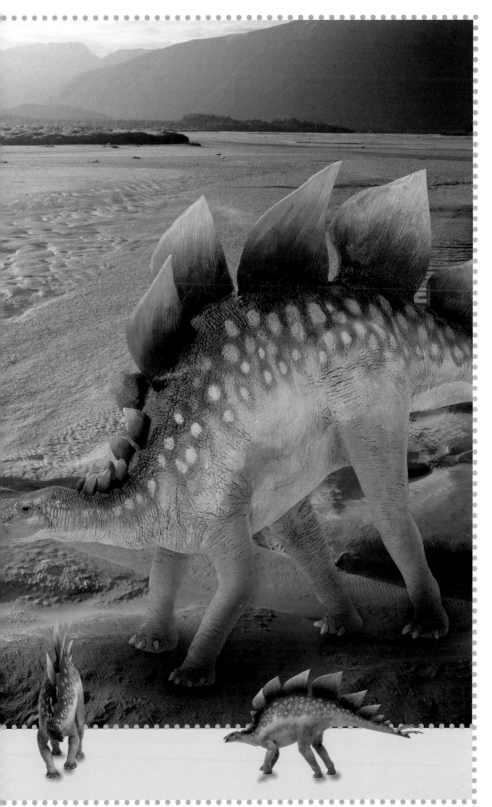

Here is the
bird-like Gallimimus
[GAL-uh-MIME-us].
It has thin legs
and a beak.

leg

Gallimimus

beak

spike

Iguanodon

Here is the strong
guanodon
[ig-WAHN-oh-don].
It has a spike on
each thumb.

Here is the plant-eater,
Stegoceras
[ste-GOSS-er-us].
It has a thick skull.

skull

Stegoceras

Here is the armored
Ankylosaurus
[an-KIE-loh-SORE-us].
It has a tail club.

Ankylosaurus

28

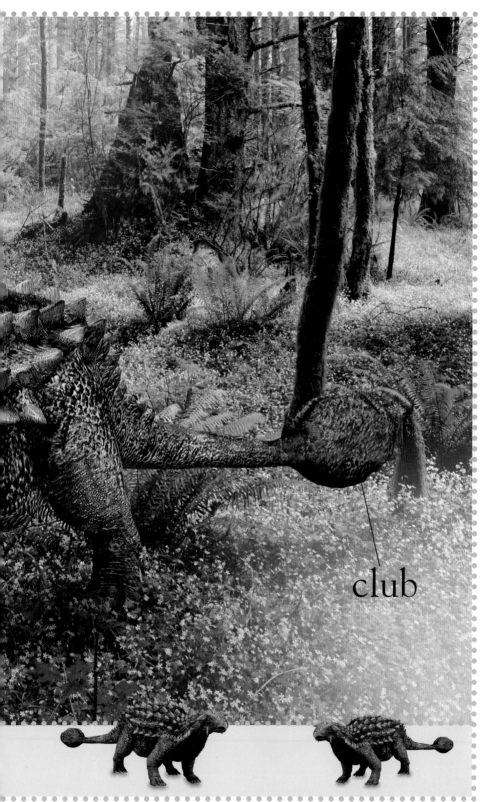

club

Which dinosaur
do you like best?
The one who is…

clever?   scary?

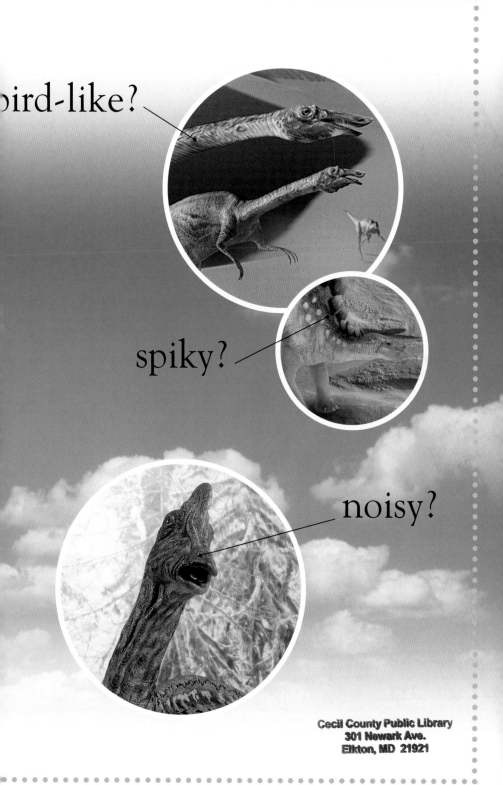

bird-like?

spiky?

noisy?

Glossary

Ankylosaurus
a plant-eating dinosaur with a tail-club

Brachiosaurus
a very tall plant-eating dinosaur

Triceratops
a plant-eating dinosaur with three horns

Tyrannosaurus
a large meat-eating dinosaur

Velociraptor
a fast and agile meat-eating dinosaur